OAK TREE

Life Cycles

Jason Cooper

Rourke

Publishing LLC

Vero Beach, Florida 32964

www.rourkepublishing.com

PHOTO CREDITS: All photos © Lynn M. Stone

Cover: *Northern oaks begin to leaf out in late April.*

Editor: Frank Sloan

Cover and page design by Nicola Stratford

Library of Congress Cataloging-in-Publication Data

Cooper, Jason, 1942-
  Oak tree / Jason Cooper.
    p. cm. — (Life cycles)
Summary: Describes the life cycle of the oak tree from flower, to acorn, to towering tree.
Includes bibliographical references.
  ISBN 1-58952-350-4 (hardcover)
  1. Oak—Life cycles—Juvenile literature. [1. Oak. 2. Trees. 3. Acorns.] I. Title.
  QK495.F14 C66 2002
  583'.46--dc21
                                                              2002006226

Printed in the USA

MP/W

Table of Contents

A live oak draped with Spanish moss stands in a damp Florida forest.

Oak Trees

Oaks are among the most common and important trees in North America. In 2001 Americans voted the oak as the national tree.

About 60 kinds of oak trees live on the mainland United States and in southern Canada. Worldwide there are more than 600 oak **species**.

Most oaks are tall, spreading trees with broad leaves. The biggest top 150 feet (45 m)! They provide shade, lumber, and a feast for wild animals.

Flowers

Oaks begin life in a small way. David Everett long ago wrote, "Tall oaks from little acorns grow." But before the acorn there was a flower. The flower produced the acorn.

A male oak flower hangs like a chain behind new spring leaves.

Acorns lie on a bed of oak leaves in autumn.

Like most other plants, oaks produce male and female flowers.

Wind carries grains of **pollen** from male flowers to the female flowers. Pollen **fertilizes** the female flowers. Over several weeks, the female flower turns into an acorn.

7

An oak seedling sprouts from an acorn.

The Oak's Seed

We know that if a tree grows acorns, it's an oak. The acorn is far more than just part of an oak tree. It is an oak's seed. And seeds **sprout** into new plants.

Acorns ripen on a northern oak in early September.

Tiny Acorns

The size of an adult plant has little to do with the size of its seeds. And so it is with oaks, even the largest of them, which stand like tall buildings. Acorns are only one-half inch (13 millimeters) to two inches (51 millimeters) in length.

A Short Life Span

In some years, one acre (.4 hectares) of oak forest may produce 700 pounds (318 kilograms) of acorns. And a single, king-sized oak could drop 15,000 acorns by itself!

Scrub jays eat acorns, and they also bury them—up to 7,000 by a single bird!

Squirrels bury acorns and find them later.

After an acorn falls, it may have a short life span. More than 150 species of birds and **mammals** eat acorns in large numbers. Some of the acorn lovers are gray and fox squirrels, bears, raccoons, wild turkeys, mice, deer, jays, woodpeckers, and certain kinds of insects.

Some buried acorns sprout and grow into oak trees.

Acorns That Sprout

An acorn that survives will sprout, sending out a root and stem. The root anchors itself in soil. The stem reaches upward. The stem grows from the food packed into the acorn.

Sometimes animals plant acorn trees. Squirrels and jays, for example, bury acorns. Later they can find and dig up most of them, but not all. Some that they miss sprout.

In winter, an oak's branches lie under a cover of snow.

Growing into an Oak Tree

As the stem grows, it uses up the food in the acorn. Then the stem's root draws food and moisture from the ground. A stem may be destroyed by shade, disease, fire, or a hungry animal. But if it survives, the stem grows into an oak tree.

The Death of an Oak

Most oaks are about 20 years old when they grow acorns. An oak may then live for another 300 or 400 years. Some oaks have lived to be 1,000 years old!

Most kinds of North American oaks live in Mexico and the South, like these live oaks in Florida.

This old trunk of an oak lies rotting on the forest floor in Missouri.

Sooner or later, even the mightiest oak falls. It may be cut down by **loggers** or cracked open by lightning. It may be weakened if gypsy moths eat its leaves. Holes in the tree may let disease enter.

Oak litter, such as acorns, leaves, and twigs, adds nutrients to the forest.

The Life Cycle Goes On

Even dead oaks are givers of life. As they rot on the forest floor, they add **nutrients** to the soil. Those nutrients provide food for other forest life—and new oaks.

**Stage 1: Oak trees
produce flowers.**

**Stage 2: The flower
becomes an acorn.
An acorn is an oak
tree's seed.**

**Stage 4: The stem may
grow into an oak tree.
The tree grows larger
and produces flowers.**

**Stage 3: The acorn may
sprout and root,
producing a stem.**

Glossary

fertilizes (FUR tuh lie zez) — makes a flower, such as an oak's, develop and grow into a seed

loggers (LOG gurz) — people who cut down trees for their wood value

mammals (MAM uhlz) — the group of warm-blooded, furry, milk-producing animals

nutrients (NEW tree entz) — things that aid healthy growth, such as vitamins and minerals

pollen (PAHL un) — dust-like grains produced by flowers to help make new flowers

species (SPEE sheez) — within a group of closely related plants, one certain kind, such as a live oak

sprout (SPROWT) — to spring up from a seed

Index

Further Reading

Morrison, Gordon. *Oak Tree.* Houghton Mifflin, 2000
Owen, Oliver S. *The Mystery of Nature: Acorn to Oak Tree.*
    ABDO, 1994

Websites to Visit

http://search.yahooligans.com/search/ligans?p=oak+tree
http://www.nwf.org/nationalwildlife/1999/nuts.html

About the Author

Jason Cooper has written several children's books about a variety of
topics for Rourke Publishing, including recent series *China Discovery*
and . Cooper travels widely to gather information for his books. Two of
his favorite travel destinations are Alaska and the Far East.